COUNCIL *on*
FOREIGN
RELATIONS

Council Special Report No. 88
September 2020

Weaponizing Digital Trade

Creating a Digital Trade Zone
to Promote Online Freedom
and Cybersecurity

Robert K. Knake

The Council on Foreign Relations (CFR) is an independent, nonpartisan membership organization, think tank, and publisher dedicated to being a resource for its members, government officials, business executives, journalists, educators and students, civic and religious leaders, and other interested citizens in order to help them better understand the world and the foreign policy choices facing the United States and other countries. Founded in 1921, CFR carries out its mission by maintaining a diverse membership, with special programs to promote interest and develop expertise in the next generation of foreign policy leaders; convening meetings at its headquarters in New York and in Washington, DC, and other cities where senior government officials, members of Congress, global leaders, and prominent thinkers come together with Council members to discuss and debate major international issues; supporting a Studies Program that fosters independent research, enabling CFR scholars to produce articles, reports, and books and hold roundtables that analyze foreign policy issues and make concrete policy recommendations; publishing *Foreign Affairs*, the preeminent journal on international affairs and U.S. foreign policy; sponsoring Independent Task Forces that produce reports with both findings and policy prescriptions on the most important foreign policy topics; and providing up-to-date information and analysis about world events and American foreign policy on its website, CFR.org.

The Council on Foreign Relations takes no institutional positions on policy issues and has no affiliation with the U.S. government. All views expressed in its publications and on its website are the sole responsibility of the author or authors.

Council Special Reports (CSRs) are concise policy briefs, produced to provide a rapid response to a developing crisis or contribute to the public's understanding of current policy dilemmas. CSRs are written by individual authors—who may be CFR fellows or acknowledged experts from outside the institution—in consultation with an advisory committee, and are intended to take sixty days from inception to publication. The committee serves as a sounding board and provides feedback on a draft report. It usually meets twice—once before a draft is written and once again when there is a draft for review; however, advisory committee members, unlike Task Force members, are not asked to sign off on the report or to otherwise endorse it. Once published, CSRs are posted on CFR.org.

For further information about CFR or this Special Report, please write to the Council on Foreign Relations, 58 East 68th Street, New York, NY 10065, or call the Communications office at 212.434.9888. Visit our website, CFR.org.

To submit a letter in response to a Council Special Report for publication on our website, CFR.org, you may send an email to publications@cfr.org. Alternatively, letters may be mailed to us at: Publications Department, Council on Foreign Relations, 58 East 68th Street, New York, NY 10065. Letters should include the writer's name, postal address, and daytime phone number. Letters may be edited for length and clarity, and may be published online. Please do not send attachments. All letters become the property of the Council on Foreign Relations and will not be returned. We regret that, owing to the volume of correspondence, we cannot respond to every letter.

CONTENTS

FOREWORD

The fight is on to determine the internet's future. Some have argued the world is heading toward a "splinternet," with the United States championing an open internet while China and Russia dominate a more regulated internet. Still others believe that authoritarian countries are unlikely to cut themselves off from the global internet and will thus focus on controlling most of the content that enters their borders. Although the contours are up for debate, the nature of the internet is clearly changing, and national governments are increasingly intervening to determine what data is allowed to flow within their borders, what data can be collected on their citizens, and where that data can be stored.

Within this context, Robert K. Knake, a senior fellow for cyber policy at the Council on Foreign Relations, looks at how the United States can best preserve its interests on the internet. Unless the United States puts forward a compelling vision that can compete with the Chinese and Russian model and gets its allies to sign on, Knake concludes that China will dominate the global internet. This would be a world in which an internet that limits privacy, promotes censorship, and supports the surveillance state is more common than not.

Knake argues the best path for the United States is to work with its democratic partners (i.e., its allies) to embed their values within digital trade, linking digital trade with promoting an open internet. The way to do so is to form a digital trade zone that ties the adoption of democratic values online to access to digital markets. This would entail negotiating a digital trade agreement that sets common standards and practices and excludes those countries that do not abide by these standards. To put it bluntly, Knake calls on the United States to weaponize its digital trade relationships to create a system that promotes its preference for internet governance. The United States and its like-minded partners would, in essence, be forcing countries to choose between maintaining access to their markets or embracing China's model.

Knake provides a road map for establishing this digital trade zone, recommending that the United States and other members build upon recent free trade agreements to set rules of the road on digital trade and data localization. Importantly, members would agree to establish privacy protections for all citizens of member states. Members would also introduce tariffs on digital goods from nonmember states, jointly sanction nonmembers that participate in banned activities, invest in an effort to improve global cyber hygiene and cybersecurity, and pledge not to conduct signals intelligence on other members or interfere in their democratic processes.

Provocatively, Knake calls for members of this trade zone to end their reliance on nonmembers for hardware and software with national security implications. Such a "democratic digital supply chain," as he terms it, would further incentivize countries to join the bloc. Interestingly, faced with the prospect of being excluded from a large digital trade zone, China could also be pressured to change its behavior. In order for this plan to work, members would have to collaboratively introduce a degree of industrial planning to ensure all of the most important technologies can be produced within the bloc. Although industrial planning of any sort might be anathema to many members—including the United States—calls to decouple the United States from China in strategic areas have increased in recent years and have intensified in the wake of the COVID-19 pandemic, making such a policy proposal timely.

Knake makes a persuasive case for the United States to use more of the tools in its arsenal—from tariffs to sanctions and market access—to promote its interests and values on the internet. As he rightly notes, it is probably no longer realistic to work toward an internet that is both open and global. Instead, he asserts the United States should respond to the challenge that China presents in internet governance and focus on working with allies to preserve an open internet that connects the digital economies of democratic countries.

In its recommendations, this report demonstrates that one of America's most important advantages over China and Russia is its network of allies. Promoting an alternative internet governance model would be much more difficult, more likely impossible, without these like-minded allies and partners. I imagine some (especially the most ardent free traders) could disagree with a few of the policy prescriptions in this report. Nonetheless, marrying digital trade with internet governance is a bold new idea that deserves serious consideration.

I end with one additional thought. Knake's partner- and ally-centric approach to internet governance lends itself to other global challenges, including climate change. It already exists in the trade realm. The goal may be global (i.e., universal governance), but requiring a global consensus as has been the case in World Trade Organization negotiations and previous climate talks is a recipe for failure or at most modest accomplishment. The alternative of working with like-minded countries can lead to an acceptable outcome and, with the passage of time, one that forms the basis for a more universal approach.

Richard N. Haass
President
Council on Foreign Relations
September 2020

ACKNOWLEDGMENTS

Digital trade, internet governance, and cybersecurity are tightly bound together in the real world but in policy circles are treated as entirely different subjects. In writing this report, I attempted to bring all three together out of a belief that the problems in any one space cannot be solved without solving problems in the others. Although the views expressed in this report are my own, my work has been shaped by many others who were willing to share their expertise, experience, and time with me. I relied on an impressive group of advisory committee members who in short order were able to school me on the finer points of digital trade negotiations, the minutiae of international legal assistance, and a dozen other topics. All did so during the difficult first months of the COVID-19 pandemic, often while juggling toddlers on their laps. For that I thank them. In particular, I thank Sanjay Parekh and Ben Dean for providing detailed comments on the draft that corrected important facts, added context, and challenged many of my early conclusions. As always, Adam Segal's edits were essential to creating a clear structure, smoothing the language, and sorting out the logic. For those efforts, I thank him. The *Net Politics* blog proved an invaluable resource; the best analysis of the outcomes of internet government forum meetings, often from foreign writers, can be found on *Net Politics*. Connor Fairman provided research assistance and a deft hand at editing the initial draft. Finally, I could not have completed this project without the help of Megan Stifel, my longtime friend and collaborator, who graciously agreed to serve as chair of the advisory committee, helped me recruit most of the members, and moderated the advisory committee meeting with aplomb.

Robert K. Knake

INTRODUCTION

The global internet is splitting apart. China, Russia, and other authoritarian regimes are working to limit what information flows in and out of their national borders while constantly surveilling internet users inside their networks. Meanwhile, China and Russia are leading efforts at the United Nations to fundamentally reengineer how the internet works and is governed to fit their Orwellian visions. For its part, Europe is heading off in its own direction, with the European Union (EU) strengthening its privacy and content moderation requirements, targeting the practices of U.S.-based technology giants. If the United States is unable to develop a competing vision, a decade from now the internet as we know it will no longer be recognizable. Not only would the United States have lost the economic value from being the global driver of digital trade and innovation, but much of the world's population would also have been mired in a web of censorship and surveillance woven by China's state-owned enterprises. In this sense, the stakes go far beyond the internet and will doubtless affect the global balance of power.

Although many efforts are underway to promote digital freedom, establish norms for state conduct in cyberspace, and address the harmful consequences of the cross-border free flow of data, these efforts are largely uncoordinated, resulting in ad hoc measures that do not create mechanisms for managing the next product of concern. More important, they lack the incentives necessary to encourage better behavior— failing to protect citizens' rights online or harboring cross-border cybercriminals has few consequences. To combat these trends, the United States should shift its diplomatic efforts from promoting a global, open internet to preserving an open internet that connects the digital economies of democratic countries.

The time to pursue a digital trade agreement that would preserve the flow of cross-border digital trade, while taking steps to address the negative effects of an open internet, is now. Trade negotiators are moving rapidly to stop countries from putting in place national laws to address cybercrime. Yet efforts at promoting digital trade will be successful only if they seriously attempt to cooperatively address cybercrime, censorship, and privacy concerns. By tying digital trade—the cross-border exchange of digital products and services—to the promotion of the free exchange of information and efforts to control the harmful side effects of an open internet, the United States and its allies can create a compelling alternative to the authoritarian vision of a tightly controlled network. In short, the United States should weaponize its digital trade relationships to create a system of incentives and penalties that will promote security hand in hand with democratic values on the internet.

No matter what the United States does, there will be a Chinese-dominated internet. The open question is whether China dominates the global internet or China competes with an open internet supported by democratic nations. The United States has a short window to draw Europe in and create a competing vision that would attract fence-sitters such as Brazil, India, and Indonesia, which have democratic traditions and are wary of Chinese hegemony on the web. If the United States can create a "digital trade zone" that rewards countries that join it and abide by its rules, many other nations could choose this vision over a future in which China dominates their countries and their people are subject to censorship and surveillance. If the digital trade zone grows strong enough, China might see more benefit to cooperative engagement than to continued disruptive behavior.

A FRAGMENTING INTERNET

In 2018, former Google CEO Eric Schmidt predicted that the internet would split into two: one dominated by the United States and its tech giants (Google, Microsoft, Apple, Facebook) and one dominated by China (Tencent, Alibaba, Baidu, Xiaomi).[1] Not to be outdone, the *New York Times* editorial board predicted that the internet would split into three networks, concluding that Europe's divergent approach from the United States on privacy issues would lead to a European Union network.[2] This trend toward fragmentation is unlikely to result in a series of totally separate national networks that do not communicate with one another. Abandonment of the internet protocol suite is unlikely, though China has proposed both a new suite of protocols and a new domain name system, both of which would tighten state control. Yet even the most authoritarian regimes (excepting North Korea) are likely to want vast quantities of data to flow across their systems—they just want to decide what data flows and see to whom it flows. Except during war or periods of internal unrest, no country is likely to see completely severing itself from the global internet as being in its interest.

What is clearly happening is a move toward an internet in which geography ultimately determines what data is allowed to flow. National borders were at first irrelevant to the internet. Over the past twenty years, they have become legally important. Current trends suggest that over the next twenty years states will place technical controls at national borders to limit what data flows in and out of their country. Although the internet was not designed to respect national borders or differentiate between one country's laws and another's, governments began to place legal restrictions on senders and receivers of digital information and digital goods and services more than twenty years ago. Germany and France carried over from the real world their laws against distributing Nazi materials and selling Nazi artifacts. If it was a crime to sell *Mein Kampf* in a bookstore, it was also a crime to sell it on Amazon or display it online to German citizens. Executives at internet companies, fearing arrest should they ever land at Charles de Gaulle international airport, learned how to use geolocation to determine whether they could lawfully display content to a viewer in the country where they were shown to be located. They could also prevent goods from being shipped to countries in which their sale was prohibited. Of course, businesses also found that it was in their interest to shape content based on location, delivering more relevant news or search results based on where they believed users were located. As Tim Wu and Jack Goldsmith pointed out in their book *Who Controls the Internet?*, the idea of a "borderless world" online was always more of an illusion than reality.[3]

The divisions between the United States and Europe have grown over the past decade as evidence of U.S. signals intelligence activities has come to light and as U.S. technology giants have solidified their grasp on the digital realm. Disclosures by Edward Snowden and others have shown that the National Security Agency and other arms of the U.S. intelligence community have collected vast troves of data on adversaries and allies alike. Meanwhile, European leaders have become increasingly apprehensive about the hold Facebook, Google, Microsoft, and other tech giants have on the digital lives of their citizens as well as envious of these foreign companies' market share. The European Union has made efforts to secure the privacy of its citizens' data from commercial interests while working to increase access to this data by local law enforcement, even when that data is stored a world away. The threat of data localization—requirements to keep data on a citizen stored in the home country of that citizen—hangs in the air, threatening cross-border digital trade. As Anupam Chander, a professor at Georgetown University Law Center, puts it, "Data localization is the nemesis of digital trade."[4]

Some progress has been made on data localization thanks in part to the success of Europe's General Data Protection Regulation (GDPR), which came into force in May 2018 and has become the de facto standard for global privacy regulations. GDPR sets rules for the privacy protection of EU citizens, gives these citizens certain rights over their data, and establishes strong enforcement mechanisms. It also sets a notification standard for data breaches involving personal information. Crucially, GDPR is extraterritorial in nature, meaning that it applies globally to any business that holds data on European citizens.

Notwithstanding the progress from GDPR, the protection of citizen data abroad and access to data by authorities remain issues, as does the taxation of digital goods and services. France has moved to impose a tax on U.S. tech giants (though it could be removed if an Organization for Economic Cooperation and Development effort to set common rules on digital taxation moves forward).[5] In March, the European Union issued a new strategy for the digital economy that calls for achieving "technological sovereignty" to end reliance on U.S. software, hardware, and services, including by creating a European cloud infrastructure that U.S. companies do not own or control.[6]

Beyond using legal means to shape internet content, borders are shifting from places where laws change to places where countries are implementing technical controls. Until recently, in most countries data flowed freely across national borders, filtered out at the corporate or individual level. Now countries are moving to preemptively restrict and shape the flow of data at national borders. China is the leader in this regard, with Russia following close behind. China operates what is known as the Great Firewall, a system of inspection points both internal and at gateways to the rest of the world that surveils internet use by Chinese citizens and blocks access to content deemed unlawful. Iran operates its National Information Network, which allows it to censor all content on the network and shut off external and internal data flows in times of unrest. China has exported its know-how to Russia, which is busy testing Runet, its so-called sovereign internet that will allow it to cut off traffic to the rest of the world. Russia has backed its technical efforts with a series of laws that make it a crime to publish what the state judges to be "fake news" or to criticize the government.[7] China has also assisted dozens of other countries that would like to emulate its system of controls.[8]

Together, China and Russia have assembled a bloc of like-minded nations that are pressing their vision for the internet in the United Nations. In December, a Russia-backed resolution to create a working group charged with developing a new cybercrime treaty passed with overwhelming support from non-Western countries.[9] The treaty would center internet governance within the United Nations, make governments the primary arbiters of the future of the internet, and, most troublingly, broadly define cybercrime so as to capture online speech that is protected in many democratic countries. Given this renewed push, the United States should work to mend the emerging rift with Europe on digital issues and create a compelling vision and attractive market that will draw in democratic countries around the globe.

TOWARD A NEW APPROACH TO INTERNET GOVERNANCE

Many countries will be pulled toward China's model of internet control no matter what the United States does. China's model is inherently appealing to authoritarian governments. But China's draw as a center of the global digital economy is not a foregone conclusion. Democratic nations, if they can unify as a bloc, can present a compelling alternative. Such action requires abandoning the hope that democratic values naturally spread through the internet. U.S. policy should move on from approaches that seek to find common ground with authoritarian regimes. Efforts through the United Nations and other global forums have never moved forward because Chinese and Russian delegates are fundamentally opposed to a liberal-democratic view of how the internet should work. Instead of working through global intergovernmental models, the United States should pursue a values-based approach that would create a digital trade zone with common standards and practices compatible with democratic values and then limit access to the digital markets within this zone to those countries that abide by these standards and practices. Such a digital trade zone should be constructed incrementally, building on existing frameworks.

BUILDING ON DIGITAL TRADE AGREEMENTS

President Donald J. Trump signed the U.S.-Mexico-Canada Agreement (USMCA) into law in January 2020, replacing the 1990s-era North American Free Trade Agreement (NAFTA).[10] Although most of the interest in USMCA has centered on the auto and agricultural industries, USMCA contains important provisions on digital trade, including expanded intellectual property protections, anti-spam laws, penalties for the theft of trade secrets (including through cyber theft), protecting cloud companies against lawsuits for user-generated content, and prohibiting governments from requesting source code for market access. Most critically, it maintains the free flow of digital trade across borders and bans data localization.

In many respects, USMCA can serve as a model for the digital trade zone; yet in others it is woefully lacking. USMCA does not include any form of mandatory privacy protections, nor does it include any means for consumers to enforce protection laws across borders. It does not require that holders of data meet a base-level data protection standard. In all, USMCA's digital trade chapter lacks the mechanisms to coordinate action on the downsides of digital trade. USMCA is unlikely to improve privacy for users, simplify cross-border law enforcement investigations, or even reduce spam. Yet the framework set out in USMCA (borrowed heavily from the Trans-Pacific Partnership) can be built upon. Japan and the European Union have also laid the groundwork for a digital trade zone under their Economic Partnership Agreement, which includes a chapter on electronic commerce that, among other things, prohibits tariffs on digital goods.[11]

ADDRESSING CROSS-BORDER CRIME

The Clarifying Lawful Overseas Use of Data (CLOUD) Act has, for a time at least, kept Europe from moving forward on data localization requirements by regulating cross-border data access requests.[12] The law gives the president the authority to enter into agreements with other countries to allow access to the content of communications in criminal investigations. The new system upends the cumbersome diplomatic process of handling foreign requests for investigative support through mutual legal assistance treaties (MLATs).

The CLOUD Act allows countries with strong rule of law and a democratic tradition to directly request data on their citizens from U.S.-based cloud providers without going through the MLAT process. Requests for data on U.S. citizens must still go through the MLAT process to be reviewed by the U.S. Department of Justice and obtain a warrant against probable cause standards. To date, only the United Kingdom has entered into an agreement with the United States under the CLOUD Act; however, Australia has begun negotiations, and the European Union has begun discussions on behalf of member states.[13]

For a country to be able to obtain data under the CLOUD Act, the attorney general must certify, with the concurrence of the secretary of state, that the laws of the country in question afford protections for privacy and civil liberty (in short, Iran need not apply). The law also provides a mechanism for Congress to object to any such certification within ninety days. Privacy protections could be strengthened in the act, but overall the act can serve as a strong basis for how a digital trade zone could prevent data localization from taking root.

Building on the CLOUD Act, the digital trade zone should establish principles for privacy and civil liberties protections and a process for determining whether proposed member states abide by those principles. Initially, that process should involve founding member states assessing each other and require consensus among all members that each country meets the requirements to join. After this initial round, the treaty organization would be responsible for assessing new applicant nations, presenting decisions to be affirmed by a majority (or some higher threshold) of members.

The effort can also build on the Council of Europe Convention on Cybercrime (known as the Budapest Convention). The Budapest Convention established many of the fundamental rules necessary to address cross-border cybercrime. It lacks only two things: carrots and sticks. The Budapest Convention provides no tangible benefits to countries that join, has weak mechanisms for coordinating to address cybercrime, and has no built-in mechanisms to punish members that do not abide by its rules; moreover, it has no tools for imposing costs on nonmembers, which impose most of the costs of cybercrime on member states. What it has done is establish, from a normative perspective, interstate obligations to assist on cybercrime. This valuable work spanning three decades can be built upon, adding in the missing mechanisms to encourage cooperative action.

CREATING A GLOBAL PRIVACY FRAMEWORK

Beyond law enforcement cooperation, the accord should also address the privacy rights of all citizens from member states. Although its implementation has had its difficulties, GDPR can serve as the basis for required national privacy legislation among members. Although the law in many ways draws a line in the sand between the United States and Europe, it has also become a global standard with the potential to be more unifying than dividing. GDPR has inspired a series of countries, including Brazil, India, Japan, South Korea, and Thailand, to follow suit with their own privacy protection laws.

GDPR could in fact be one of the more important efforts to stem the push toward data localization. By creating a legal framework with global reach in GDPR, Europe has provided a blueprint for how data can be stored globally while being protected by local laws. The European Union has recognized that Japan is offering sufficient protection of personal data under GDPR standards and has agreed to a framework for mutual and smooth transfer of personal data that allows data protected under GDPR to flow freely between the two countries.[14] This outcome is one of the first tangible steps toward realizing former Japanese Prime Minister Shinzo Abe's push to develop a global set of rules for data governance with the goal of promoting the "free flow of data with trust."[15] Abe proposed the Osaka Track at the Group of Twenty last year to further develop the concept.

Julie Brill, a former commissioner of the Federal Trade Commission, now employed at Microsoft, has advocated for the United States to adopt GDPR. "For American businesses," she argues, "interoperability between U.S. law and GDPR will reduce the cost and complexity of compliance by ensuring that companies don't have to build separate systems to meet differing—and even conflicting—requirements for privacy protection in the countries where they do business."[16] Moving from a situation in which Europe is able to compel U.S. companies to meet privacy requirements for its citizens to one in which the United States and other democratic countries have adopted the same requirements and enforcement mechanisms will strengthen trust in those protections as implemented by U.S. companies. Creating a trade zone that explicitly requires countries to meet the obligations of GDPR could do more than anything to smooth the flow of digital trade.

To address common security concerns and provide an added incentive for joining the trade zone, member states should agree to jointly end reliance on hardware and software from nonmember states in critical infrastructure and national security applications. The challenge with implementing this approach now is that there are few alternatives for 5G networks and none provide the same capability or can be purchased at the same price point. Thus, the current effort to block Huawei and replace it has hit a stumbling block. To address this challenge, member countries need to create a market for trusted technology products and services that will attract market entrants.

Particularly for developing countries, tying digital trade to the manufacturing of the hardware that makes digital life possible can create an attractive market opportunity. Aligning manufacturing of critical electronics and digital trade would provide a significant incentive for countries to join the digital trade zone and set in place plans to replace Chinese-manufactured equipment, thereby eliminating significant risk from current global supply chains.

Chris Krebs, director of the Cybersecurity and Infrastructure Security Agency at the Department of Homeland Security, has articulated a multipart test that the Trump administration used in deciding to ban the Russian antivirus company Kaspersky from federal agencies and to thwart the Chinese telecommunications firm Huawei's entrance into the U.S. market under an executive order.[17] That test includes three components and asks these questions:

- Does the technology when deployed provide access to or support critical national security and critical infrastructure operations?

- Does the company operate in a jurisdiction that compels telecommunications companies and technology companies to comply with requests from intelligence services?

- Is there a known relationship between the intelligence service and company management?

Both Kaspersky and Huawei failed the test. The case against Kaspersky is based on Russian laws that would compel it to cooperate with Russian intelligence, the functionality of its antivirus software (which sends sensitive data back to the company's offices in Russia and introduces other technical risks), and the potential for Russia's Federal Security Service to coerce Kaspersky's cooperation in exchange for being granted the required licenses to operate its business. With respect to Huawei, China's 2017 National Intelligence Law and 2014 Counterespionage Law compel companies to cooperate with the Chinese government. In addition, Krebs states, the Chinese government is heavily involved in Huawei. Finally, the U.S. government claims that it has discovered so-called backdoors in Huawei's 4G network equipment, leading it to believe that 5G equipment will be riddled with intentionally placed vulnerabilities that China can exploit at will. As the Council on Foreign Relations' Jerome Cohen put it,

> There is no way Huawei can resist any order from the [People's Republic of China] Government or the Chinese Communist Party to do its bidding in any context, commercial or otherwise. Huawei would have to turn over all requested data and perform whatever other surveillance activities are required. . . . Not only is this mandated by existing legislation but, more important, also by political reality and the organizational structure and operation of the Party-State's economy. The Party is embedded in Huawei and controls it.[18]

While the test Krebs provided is straightforward, it also would include a large set of technologies if applied more broadly. To encourage the development of supply chains that do not run through China, member states of a digital trade zone would need to ensure through joint industrial planning that the most important technologies for national security applications are produced within member states. Doing so could also provide a powerful incentive for drawing in countries that initially wish to stay unaligned with either the digital trade zone or the emerging Chinese digital hegemony. India, for one, amid the pandemic, is moving to make itself a hub for electronic manufacturing while pressing forward with plans to require data localization.[19] The incentive to become a manufacturing hub for digital trade zone companies as well as strengthened measures for access to and protection of Indian citizen data under the accord would likely prove sufficient to counter its data localization plans. Industrial planning has fallen out of fashion, but creating the capacity for trade zone members to identify critical products and produce them within the trade zone is necessary. Absent the ability to produce these critical products inside the trade zone, the coalition should look for opportunities to produce those goods outside China.

For its part, China could press its case in the World Trade Organization (WTO), arguing that efforts to exclude its technology products from markets are an abuse of the national security exception allowed under WTO rules. The Chinese delegation to the WTO has already made this argument with respect to Trump's executive order on Huawei but has yet to formally file a complaint with the WTO.[20] If China chose to do so and the WTO agreed that U.S. rules were in fact abusive, the WTO would have the authority to approve similar restrictions on U.S. technology products or other coalition member technology products but would not have the authority to force the United States or its partner countries to end the practice. As written, the national security exemption provides broad authority for countries to determine what is and is not a national security concern.[21] In its first ruling on a complaint alleging abuse of the exemption by Russia over blocking the transit of Ukrainian goods across its territory, the WTO upheld Russia's use of the exemption.[22]

RECOMMENDATIONS

The U.S. government should work with other democratic nations, the technology industry, nonprofits, academia, and user groups to create a digital trade zone with rules that govern content moderation, data localization, cross-border cybercrime, and obligations to assist during cyberattacks. It should then establish the organizations and mechanisms necessary to implement these agreements. By tying access to the digital trade zone to obligations for cybersecurity, privacy, and law enforcement cooperation, the United States and its democratic allies can create a compelling alternative to authoritarian visions for the internet. In doing so, the United States and its allies can force countries to choose between access to their markets or tight control of the internet in the Chinese model, thereby creating the kind of leverage that has been missing from U.S. efforts to promote an open, interoperable, secure, and reliable internet. Tariffs on digital goods from outside the trade zone should be used, at least in part, to fund joint cybersecurity efforts within the zone.

ESTABLISH A TREATY ORGANIZATION TO COORDINATE CYBERSECURITY AND LAW ENFORCEMENT EFFORTS

Missing from existing bilateral efforts on digital trade, law enforcement cooperation, cybersecurity, and privacy is a trusted, independent third party to mediate disputes, rate compliance, and coordinate action. The first step toward making digital trade a lever for addressing the harmful side effects of cross-border data flows is to establish an organization for this purpose. Provisions in USMCA direct the three countries to consider creating a forum to promote cooperation on digital trade issues. Although USMCA's cybersecurity requirements are decidedly toothless, the list of topics the forum covers does include security matters. Working with Canada and Mexico, the United States could establish such an organization under the auspices of USMCA, work out its functions, and then seek to draw in other countries to participate.

CREATE A SHARED TARIFF AND SANCTIONS POLICY

For the digital trade zone to be effective, digital trade should freely flow among member states, but member states should also limit digital trade with nonmember states. Some form of tariff on all digital goods from nonmember states entering the digital trade zone is likely warranted. Trade zone members should also agree to jointly sanction nonmember states that harbor cybercriminals or participate in banned activities. The threat of coordinated sanctions would provide a strong mechanism to change the behavior of nonmember states. Coordinated sanctions should begin with warnings and narrowly target specific actors. Punitive measures under this policy could include coordinated efforts to deny access to companies in uncooperative countries that are causing harm inside the digital trade zone. In some cases, countries that currently abide by the practices required for membership could decide not to align with the U.S.-led coalition so as to maintain access to Chinese markets and Chinese technologies. Some mechanism may be necessary to encourage continued good behavior but not grant the full benefit of membership.

CREATE SUSTAINED FUNDING FOR COLLECTIVE EFFORTS

Cybersecurity has proved a poor charitable cause. Against other pressing issues such as climate change, poverty alleviation, and global health, cybersecurity has not attracted significant support from individual donors or foundations. Many of the protocols necessary to secure cyberspace do not benefit individual companies and are therefore not suited to marketplace solutions. Organizations such as the Shadowserver Foundation, which has played an important role in many cybercrime takedown operations, are struggling to find support to keep their operations going.[23] Funding organizations that have stepped in to provide support have done so with finite time horizons. Yet cybersecurity is an ongoing problem that is unlikely to ever be definitively solved. Thus, an ongoing stream of funding to improve global cyber hygiene, build cybersecurity capacity in developing countries, and coordinate international law enforcement investigations and takedown operations is necessary.

Efforts such as the Global Forum on Cyber Expertise, the Cyber-security Tech Accord, and the Digital Geneva Convention, which seek support from both technology companies and governments, are good models. Under this thinking, the agreement should require each member state to contribute annual payments to the treaty organization to support these efforts. Dues should be based on a combination of per capita gross domestic product (GDP) and total GDP so that the largest, richest countries pay the most dues and the smallest, poorest signatories pay the least. The costs of dues would be covered by tariffs on digital goods sold into the zone from companies located outside it. These funds could also be used to support efforts by developing countries to replace existing Chinese technology in their critical networks.

INVOLVE NONGOVERNMENTAL STAKEHOLDERS

In shaping and implementing the digital trade zone and its enforcement mechanisms, nongovernmental stakeholders should crucially be included. Although the U.S. government's efforts to remove itself from the operation and governance of the network have shaped much of the history of the internet, only governments can establish rules to govern interstate trade. However, for the digital trade zone to achieve its goals, individual and corporate user groups, internet service providers (ISPs), content service providers (CSPs), software and hardware makers, and cybersecurity companies will all need to be involved. Although the digital trade zone will undoubtedly place new requirements on private companies, voluntary efforts in support of its development should also be encouraged. For companies organized and operating outside of member states, treaty instruments should set the terms under which such companies could be brought into the fold. For instance, a Russian hosting provider should be able to meet applicable requirements of stewardship, such as responsiveness to takedown requests and implementation of cybersecurity standards, and then could be exempted from tariffs on its digital goods sold within the trade zone. Such a mechanism would incentivize individual companies to adhere to the digital trade zone's rules and pressure their governments to clean up their acts.

CLEAN UP THE OPEN WEB

Treaty mechanisms should also include an organization to coordinate efforts to improve cybersecurity hygiene. Although private companies have begun to use security scoring to rate their supply chain members and press them to improve security, a wider effort coordinated at the international and national levels is likely necessary. The organization should take responsibility for rating countries on their cybersecurity hygiene efforts so that a name-and-shame effect can take hold. Beyond simply scanning and rating, the treaty organization should also fund initiatives to promote the implementation of more secure protocols. In many developing countries, training and technical resources could be necessary to improve cyber hygiene. A crucial part of this effort should be a sustained, coordinated effort to dismantle the infrastructure used by cybercriminals. The organization should fund national and international efforts to address these challenges.

KEEP ICANN INDEPENDENT, BUT PRESSURE IT TO CLEAN UP DOMAIN SPACE

The Barack Obama administration moved forward with long-stalled plans to sever the contract between the U.S. Commerce Department and the Internet Corporation for Assigned Names and Numbers (ICANN), which carries out the management of the internet's root zone, the system for assigning internet protocol (IP) addresses and domain names. Doing so tamped down calls by China, Russia, and others to transition these functions to a UN-designated body (that they could then control), but ICANN has done little to address cybercriminals' abuse of the domain name system. Cybercriminals use the domain name system to command and control botnets, set up fake websites to distribute malware, and advertise fraud. ICANN should be pressured to strengthen identity requirements for registering websites, improve systems for abuse reporting, and punish registrars that cater to criminal entities.

FIX NOTICE, TAKEDOWN, AND SINKHOLING

The treaty should establish strong mechanisms to provide notice of cyber threats emanating from networks and systems, oversee the elimination of these threats, and create consequences for companies that do not cooperate in these efforts. Abuse-reporting systems on the internet are broken. For cybersecurity threats such as malware distribution and distributed denial of service attacks, companies lack incentives to respond rapidly to notices and requests or, in some cases, to better police their infrastructure to prevent it from being used in the first place. On the other side of the equation, notice and takedown provisions for abuse of intellectual property rights are too strong, without an adequate system for appealing requests. For cybersecurity issues, the role of national computer emergency response teams is unclear. The obligations of ISPs and CSPs to address malicious activity when notified of it also remain murky. The accord should formalize systems for notification of malicious activity and enforce requirements to take down infrastructure used by malicious actors. With a system in place within the zone, treaty mechanisms should also punish bad actors operating outside the zone. The treaty should establish a coordinated system to drop traffic from companies outside the zone that are causing problems inside the zone.

BAN COVERT ELECTION INTERFERENCE AND ACCEPT A "NO SPY" PROVISION

U.S. allies in this effort, such as Germany, and countries that should be drawn in, such as Brazil, are likely to raise U.S. digital spying revealed by Edward Snowden and other leakers as evidence that the United States is itself not trustworthy in the digital domain. Although the United States was able to draw a distinction between its own spying and the kind of spying China has conducted to steal trade secrets and intellectual property to benefit its state-owned enterprises and national champion companies, that the United States was revealed to have tapped Angela Merkel's cell phone and stolen data on Brazilian oil production did not put the United States in the best light. Many countries that should be members of this coalition are known to conduct espionage against their allies, notably the United States, France, and Israel. Banning signals intelligence collection against member governments and confining espionage to softer forms of human intelligence among member states would be a reasonable compromise. Member countries should know that the ghosts in their systems are not other members of the digital trade zone. Similarly, with evidence of a global online campaign of Russian interference coming into clear view, the accord should ban member states from engaging in covert election interference. Crucially, this ban should prohibit members from engaging in covert election interference globally, not just against other member states.

LIMIT DIGITAL TRADE, NOT DATA FLOWS

Border control in cyberspace is a doomed endeavor because advanced cyber threats cannot be detected as they flow across the network. These threats hide in the streams of data that make up digital commerce. With the growth of encrypted traffic, an otherwise overwhelmingly beneficial outcome, scanning traffic at national borders for advanced threats is all but impossible. The detection of advanced threats requires presence on individual endpoints, in cloud environments, and on company networks. Even if this malicious traffic were not encrypted, differentiating between it and all other traffic on a national level is a technologically impossible task. Weakening encryption at a national level, as the British and Australian governments have proposed, would therefore do little to prevent malicious cyber activity but would weaken privacy protections for citizens. Instead of creating a bordered internet that attempts to limit access at the network level to malicious cyber actors, a better course of action is to limit access to digital markets—tax the buying and selling of digital goods for countries that are not members of the trade zone and prohibit the worst-behaving countries from selling into the trade zone entirely.

TABLE THE HARDEST ISSUES

Certain complicated issues in internet governance are unlikely to be resolved by trade negotiators and should be tabled to prevent stalling the formation of the trade zone. Trying to reach common ground on them, even among democratic states, would likely derail the overall effort to create a digital trade area. Two related issues could prove to be the most vexing: law enforcement access to encrypted data and controlling the sale of dual-use cybersecurity tools, which can be used both to test defenses and, in the wrong hands, to bypass them. These two topics have pitted the technology community against law enforcement and arms control groups, respectively. Finding common ground on these topics within domestic political processes has proved challenging; achieving a consensus among democratic states would be all but impossible. In a digital trade context, tabling these issues could prove difficult but is likely necessary to reach an agreement.

CONCLUSION

Now is a difficult time to propose anything to do with international trade. Amid the COVID-19 pandemic, long-held positions on globalization as a value generation engine for the planet are being questioned. As global supply chains fracture and many Western nations are no longer able to produce their own medical supplies and pharmaceuticals, countries are questioning the wisdom of offshoring the production of most goods. Many technology companies had already begun to recognize that the "build once, sell everywhere" mantra that had guided them through the past two decades was not going to work in the next and had started the process of disaggregating their supply chains so that Chinese manufacturers would not serve the U.S. market.

This process is now accelerating within the digital domain. After many years of courting favor with Beijing, Facebook appears to have finally abandoned hope of entering the Chinese market, and Google's plans to reenter it have been scuttled many times over. While maintaining tight control of their own digital markets, Chinese companies have rapidly gained market share in the United States and Europe. Globally, with both Huawei and ZTE, China is now the dominant telecommunications hub. Tencent is both the largest video game company and a dominant social media conglomerate. China's campaign for global domination in the digital realm has been built on its real-world Belt and Road Initiative, which is constructing infrastructure projects across Asia and Africa. These efforts are tied tightly to its Digital Silk Road initiative to build telecom infrastructure across Asia.

At present, the United States can do little to alter Chinese actions within its borders or its near abroad. Countries aligned with the Chinese vision of network and content control are unlikely to be persuaded in the near term to align with the U.S. vision of open networks and free-flowing content. In short, countries that do not respect human rights offline are unlikely to respect human rights online. By creating a democratically aligned digital free trade zone, even China might be compelled to reform its behavior so as to access this market.

Given this reality, the United States should take a new approach, and the recommendations outlined in this report can be a start. There is still an opportunity to enshrine democratic values within digital trade while also addressing the downsides of the cross-border flow of data. Digital trade can be enhanced if the mitigation strategies to the ills it creates are baked into digital trade agreements; conversely, addressing cybercrime and other digital ills that freely flow across open digital borders will only happen if these strategies are tied to digital trade. Such thinking, however, is anathema to trade negotiators, who are typically hostile to the concerns of law enforcement and actively work to limit oversight and enforcement mechanisms in trade negotiations, believing that they will encumber free trade. Yet failing to build in these mechanisms will ultimately harm the prospects of increased digital trade if threats in the digital domain are not curtailed.

Securing an open, interoperable, secure, and reliable internet against threats from authoritarian regimes will likely require abandoning hope that such a network can be global. Although authoritarian regimes are unlikely to choose to cut themselves off completely from the global internet, they are taking steps to control their own networks through laws, trade restrictions, and technical means. Meanwhile, those same countries continue to wreak havoc on the networks of countries that remain open. More and more countries are being drawn into the Chinese model of state-controlled networks that limit privacy, build in the capacity for censorship, and provide the backbone for the surveillance state.

To combat this trend, the United States and its allies should form a digital trade zone that ties the adoption of democratic values online to access to digital markets. Being part of this digital trade zone should require member countries to commit to being good partners in improving cybersecurity so that the ill effects of cross-border digital trade do not undermine the value of that trade. By doing so, the United States and its allies can create a compelling alternative to the authoritarian web.

ENDNOTES

1. Lora Kolodny, "Former Google CEO Predicts the Internet Will Split in Two—and One Part Will Be Led by China," CNBC, September 20, 2018, http://cnbc.com /2018/09/20/eric-schmidt-ex-google-ceo-predicts-internet-split-china.html.

2. The Editorial Board, "There May Soon Be Three Internets. America's Won't Necessarily Be the Best." *New York Times*, October 15, 2018, http://nytimes.com /2018/10/15/opinion/internet-google-china-balkanization.html.

3. Jack Goldsmith and Tim Wu, *Who Controls the Internet? Illusions of a Borderless World* (New York: Oxford University Press, 2008).

4. Anupam Chander, "The Coming North American Digital Trade Zone," *Net Politics* (blog), October 9, 2018, http://cfr.org/blog/coming-north-american-digital-trade-zone.

5. Elizabeth Schulze, "US and France Have Reached a Deal on Digital Tax, Macron Says," CNBC, August 26, 2019, http://cnbc.com/2019/08/27/france-and-us-reach-draft -compromise-on-french-digital-tax.html.

6. "Europe Investing in Digital," European Commission, March 9, 2020, http://ec.europa .eu/digital-single-market/en/europe-investing-digital.

7. Shannon Van Sant, "Russia Criminalizes the Spread of Online News Which 'Disrespects' the Government," NPR, March 18, 2019, http://npr.org/2019/03/18 /704600310/russia-criminalizes-the-spread-of-online-news-which-disrespects -the-government.

8. Paresh Dave, "China Exports Its Restrictive Internet Policies to Dozens of Countries: Report," Reuters, November 1, 2018, http://reuters.com/article/us-global-internet -surveillance/china-exports-its-restrictive-internet-policies-to-dozens-of-countries -report-idUSKCN1N63KE.

9. *Countering the Use of Information and Communications Technologies for Criminal Purposes*, Report of the Seventy-Fourth Session, UN General Assembly, Agenda Item 107, November 25, 2019, http://undocs.org/A/74/401.

10. Ana Swanson and Jim Tankersley, "Trump Just Signed the U.S.M.C.A. Here's What's in the New NAFTA." *New York Times*, January 29, 2020, http://nytimes.com /2020/01/29/business/economy/usmca-deal.html.

11. "Annex to the Proposal for a Council Decision on the Conclusion of the Economic Partnership Agreement Between the European Union and Japan," European Commission, April 18, 2018, http://eur-lex.europa.eu/legal-content/EN/TXT/?uri=CELEX:52018PC0192#document2.

12. Aravind Swaminathan, Robert Loeb, Brian P. Goldman, and Emily S. Tabatabai, "The CLOUD Act, Explained," Orrick, April 6, 2018, http://orrick.com/en/Insights/2018/04/The-CLOUD-Act-Explained.

13. Jennifer Daskal and Peter Swire, "The U.K.-U.S. CLOUD Act Agreement Is Finally Here, Containing New Safeguards," *Lawfare*, October 8, 2019, http://lawfareblog.com/uk-us-cloud-act-agreement-finally-here-containing-new-safeguards.

14. "The Framework for Mutual and Smooth Transfer of Personal Data Between Japan and the European Union Has Come Into Force," Personal Information Protection Commission of Japan, January 23, 2019, http://www.ppc.go.jp/en/aboutus/roles/international/cooperation/20190123.

15. Satoshi Sugiyama, "Abe Heralds Launch of 'Osaka Track' Framework for Free Cross-Border Data Flow at G20," *Japan Times*, June 28, 2019, http://japantimes.co.jp/news/2019/06/28/national/abe-heralds-launch-osaka-track-framework-free-cross-border-data-flow-g20.

16. Liam Tung, "GDPR, USA? Microsoft Says U.S. Should Match the EU's Digital Privacy Law," ZDNet, May 21, 2019, http://zdnet.com/article/gdpr-usa-microsoft-says-us-should-match-the-eus-digital-privacy-law.

17. Chris Krebs and Michael Morell, "Chris Krebs Talks With Michael Morell on 'Intelligence Matters,'" *Intelligence Matters*, June 26, 2019, http://cbsnews.com/news/transcript-chris-krebs-talks-with-michael-morell-on-intelligence-matters.

18. Arjun Kharpal, "Huawei Says It Would Never Hand Data to China's Government. Experts Say It Wouldn't Have a Choice," CNBC, March 4, 2019, http://cnbc.com/2019/03/05/huawei-would-have-to-give-data-to-china-government-if-asked-experts.html.

19. Nidhi Singal, "India to Become Electronic Manufacturing Hub, Cabinet Approves Scheme," MSN, March 21, 2020, http://msn.com/en-in/money/news/india-to-become-electronic-manufacturing-hub-cabinet-approves-scheme/ar-BB11vARW; and Mallika Singh, "RCEP Pull-Out: India Stands by Reduced Trade Deficits, Data Localisation, and Enhancing Domestic Markets," WION, November 5, 2019, http://wionews.com/india-news/rcep-pull-out-in-the-face-of-chinese-products-potentially-flooding-the-market-india-wants-to-reduce-deficits-and-keep-data-localisation-intact-260125.

20. Stephanie Nebehay, "China Hits Back at U.S. Telecom Supply Chain Order at WTO," Reuters, June 11, 2020, http://reuters.com/article/us-usa-trade-china-wto/china-hits-back-at-u-s-telecom-supply-chain-order-at-wto-idUSKBN23I32V.

21. "Article XXI: Security Exceptions," in *Analytical Index of the GATT*, World Trade Organization, http://wto.org/english/res_e/booksp_e/gatt_ai_e/art21_e.pdf.

22. William Alan Reinsch and Jack Caporal, "The WTO's First Ruling on National Security: What Does It Mean for the United States?," Center for Strategic and Security Studies, April 5, 2019, http://csis.org/analysis/wtos-first-ruling-national-security-what-does-it-mean-united-states.

23. Brian Krebs, "The Web's Bot Containment Unit Needs Your Help," *Krebs on Security*, March 16, 2020, http://krebsonsecurity.com/2020/03/the-webs-bot-containment-unit-needs-your-help.

ABOUT THE AUTHOR

Robert K. Knake is a senior fellow for cyber policy at the Council on Foreign Relations (CFR). Knake served from 2011 to 2015 as director for cybersecurity policy at the National Security Council. In this role, he was responsible for the development of presidential policy on cybersecurity and built and managed federal processes for cyber incident response and vulnerability management. Before joining government, Knake was an international affairs fellow at CFR.

Knake's publications include *The Fifth Domain: Defending Our Country, Our Companies, and Ourselves in the Age of Cyber Threats*, *Cyber War: The Next Threat to National Security and What to Do About It*, and the CFR Council Special Report *Internet Governance in an Age of Cyber Insecurity*. He has testified before Congress on cybersecurity information sharing and on the problem of attribution in cyberspace and has written and lectured extensively on cybersecurity policy. Knake holds undergraduate degrees in history and government from Connecticut College and a master's degree in public policy from the Harvard Kennedy School.

ADVISORY COMMITTEE
Weaponizing Digital Trade

Michael A. Clauser
Access Partnership

Sumon S. Dantiki
King & Spalding LLP

Benjamin Dean
Hiscox Insurance Group

Sam W. DuPont
*German Marshall Fund
of the United States*

David R. Edelman
*Massachusetts Institute
of Technology*

Kristen E. Eichensehr
*University of California,
Los Angeles School of Law*

Chris Kubecka
HypaSec

Welby J. Leaman
Walmart

Sanjay Parekh

Adam Segal, *ex officio*
Council on Foreign Relations

Megan Stifel
Global Cyber Alliance

Ricardo S. Tavares
TechPolis, Inc.

Shaarik H. Zafar
Facebook

---

www.ingramcontent.com/pod-product-compliance
Lightning Source LLC
Chambersburg PA
CBHW070818280326
41934CB00012B/3228